The KidHaven Science Library

Computers

by Roberta Baxter

KIDHAVEN PRESS
An imprint of Thomson Gale, a part of The Thomson Corporation

Detroit • New York • San Francisco • San Diego • New Haven, Conn. • Waterville, Maine • London • Munich

© 2005 Thomson Gale, a part of The Thomson Corporation.

Thomson and Star Logo are trademarks and Gale and KidHaven Press are registered trademarks used herein under license.

For more information, contact
KidHaven Press
27500 Drake Rd.
Farmington Hills, MI 48331-3535
Or you can visit our Internet site at http://www.gale.com

ALL RIGHTS RESERVED.
No part of this work covered by the copyright hereon may be reproduced or used in any form or by any means—graphic, electronic, or mechanical, including photocopying, recording, taping, Web distribution or information storage retrieval systems—without the written permission of the publisher.

LIBRARY OF CONGRESS CATALOGING-IN-PUBLICATION DATA

Baxter, Roberta, 1952–
  Computers / by Roberta Baxter.
    p. cm.—(The KidHaven science library)
  Includes bibliographical references and index.
  ISBN 0-7377-3053-6 (hard cover : alk. paper)
  1. Computers—Juvenile literature. I. Title. II. Series.
  QA76.23.B39 2005
  004—dc22

2004010946

Printed in the United States of America

Contents

Chapter 1
The Invention of Computers 4

Chapter 2
Computers at Work 14

Chapter 3
Computers for Fun 24

Chapter 4
Super Fast, Super Powerful 33

Glossary 42

For Further Exploration 43

Index 45

Picture Credits 47

About the Author 48

Chapter 1

The Invention of Computers

Computers run many of the machines that people use every day. Calculators, cars, microwave ovens, traffic signals, and CD players all rely on computer technology. Specifically, they rely on computer chips. These tiny electronic parts help keep these machines running properly. For example, a computer chip runs the clock that tells a microwave oven when to shut off. Cars also have computer chips. They control the fuel and air mixture in the engine. Machines did not always depend on computers. In fact, the first working computer was not built until the 1940s. That computer, known as ENIAC, was introduced in 1946.

Vacuum Tubes and Wires

ENIAC was not anything like the computers people use in homes, offices, and schools today. For one thing, it was enormous. It weighed 30 tons (27 metric tons) and was as large as four school buses. It also required about 500 miles (805km) of wire. The wire connected some 19,000 **vacuum tubes**.

The vacuum tubes acted like switches. In the on position, the vacuum tube allowed the flow of electrical current. In the off position, no current flowed. The switches sent information through the computer by turning electric current on and off.

ENIAC was a major advance in technology.

In 1947 an engineer fine-tunes the massive ENIAC, the world's first working computer.

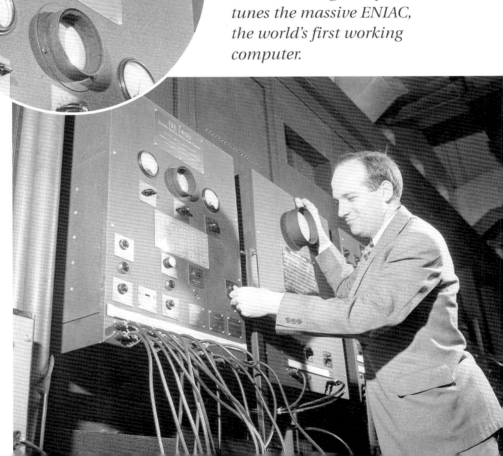

It could calculate numbers and process information much faster than a person could. It could do about 5,000 calculations per second. No person could ever manage to do this alone.

Keeping ENIAC working properly was a huge challenge. Each time a person wanted the computer to do a different type of job, the machine had to be rewired. If the job required multiplication, certain parts were wired together. If a job required division, other parts were wired together. It took hours of work to rewire the computer for just a few minutes of running time. In addition, because there were so many wires and so many connections, it was not uncommon for wires to come loose, which then had to be reconnected.

Another problem with ENIAC was the vacuum tube itself. Vacuum tubes are similar in some ways to light bulbs. Like light bulbs, they are made of glass, break easily, and burn out. Replacing broken or burned-out vacuum tubes was a huge chore. These and other problems led to new and better ways of operating computers.

Smaller and Faster

Scientists at Bell Labs in New Jersey were among those experimenting with ways to improve on vacuum tubes. They tested silicon, a chemical element commonly found in sand. In 1948, they sandwiched together layers of silicon to make a new switch called a **transistor**.

Technicians spent hours rewiring ENIAC each time they needed the computer to perform a different calculation.

A transistor is a tiny switch similar to a light switch. When the switch is on, electricity can flow through. When the switch is off, electricity cannot flow. Transistors had many advantages over vacuum tubes. Because they are solid silicon, they do not break. They are also much smaller than vacuum tubes. A computer with transistors could be made much smaller than a computer with vacuum tubes.

FIRST SILICON TRANSISTOR

Introduced in 1948, the first silicon transistors were much smaller and more durable than the vacuum tubes used in ENIAC.

Like vacuum tubes, however, transistors had to be connected to many other parts. Each transistor was hooked to wires, connectors, and other parts. All these parts made up the circuit through which an electric current could move through the machine. A single computer required 25,000 transistors, and they all had to be wired together. With so many wires and connections, loose wires were common. Just one loose wire could disrupt the entire computer.

Solving the Wire Problem

In 1958, two engineers, one in Texas and one in California, took a huge step toward solving the wire problem. They built all the parts of a circuit—transistors, wires, and connections—from a single, small piece of silicon. Because all the parts of the circuit were combined, or integrated, on one piece of silicon, they came to be known as **integrated circuits**. They are also called computer chips. Jack Kilby and Robert Noyce changed the future of computers with their invention.

Each integrated circuit had a special function. A memory chip stored data. A processor chip processed data. When these specialized chips were wired together, a computer could perform many tasks. However, most computers could still do only one type of work. A scientific computer required one set of integrated circuits, while an accounting computer required another set.

Eventually, engineers developed integrated circuits that combined both memory and processing on one, tiny chip. This chip, called a **microprocessor**, allowed a computer to do many different jobs at once. With this advance, computers could be built smaller, cheaper, and faster. Computers with microprocessors could do millions of calculations per second. Computer speeds today are measured in nanoseconds, which is one-billionth of a second.

In 1969 a computer technician studies a magnified diagram of an integrated circuit, also known as a computer chip (inset).

Software Advances

Computer chips and other physical parts of a computer are called **hardware**. All computers have hardware. Hardware alone does not make a computer, however. The programs that give instructions to the hardware are called **software**. While engineers were inventing transistors and microprocessors, computer scientists were designing software to make computers run.

Computers and people do not speak the same language. In order for people to be able to tell a computer what to do, people and computers need a common language. In the 1950s, Grace Murray Hopper designed a language that would take commands from people and turn them into a language a computer could understand. Since then, programmers have developed several different computer languages. Using these languages, programmers guide a computer through a set of actions to solve a problem or accomplish a task.

Using Computer Languages

This process is not all that different from how people accomplish everyday tasks. To make a sandwich, for example, a person first decides what kind of sandwich to make. If the decision is peanut butter, the person leaves the ham in the refrigerator and reaches for the peanut butter. The next decision may have to do with bread.

Grace Hopper (pictured) invented a computer language that allowed computers to process commands from people.

Step-by-step, decision after decision, the person makes the sandwich.

Computer programs also work step-by-step. Using computer language, step-by-step computer programs guide the computer to perform tasks.

Early computer languages such as the one written by Hopper were understood only by people with special training. New methods were needed to make it possible for anyone to use computers. Bill Gates introduced his software company, Microsoft, in 1975. Computer pioneers, Steve Jobs and Stephen Wozniak founded Apple Computers in 1976, and in 1984, produced the Macintosh with a mouse attached. These men invented the system of buttons and **icons** that are standard on computers today. By pointing and clicking with a mouse, a person can make a computer work without having to understand any computer language. These software advances made it possible for everyone to understand and use computers.

Chapter 2

Computers at Work

Computers have many uses in the workplace. Banks use computers to track money that goes into and out of accounts. Schools use computers to follow student progress and keep track of grades. Supermarkets use computers to scan bar codes and keep track of inventory. Computers help people in nearly every job and type of work.

Computers and Airplanes

People in the airline industry rely on computers for nearly everything they do. At the airport, ticket agents check each passenger's reservations on computers. Many airlines use e-tickets, or electronic tickets. These are tickets purchased by computer online. A record of these tickets exists in the airline's computer system. Passengers who use e-tickets do not need paper tickets.

While passengers are checking in, the pilot files a flight plan, listing the type of aircraft and intended route and speed. The information is entered into a computer. While the plane is in flight, the information is constantly updated.

People who work at air traffic control centers can track and communicate with hundreds of planes at one time by using computers, radar, and special software . More than 800 flights a day take off from the Baltimore/Washington International Airport. Computers display information from each plane. This is how the air traffic controllers know which planes are going to Chicago and which ones are headed for Dallas or other cities. During the flight, the plane flying to Chicago is tracked by four controllers. The ground controller

Computers help air traffic controllers coordinate the movements of hundreds of planes at once.

guides the plane to a landing using the information displayed on a computer.

As a plane approaches for landing, computer software calculates the number of planes approaching and leaving the airport at the same time and the number of available runways. It then develops a plan to land all the planes safely, quickly, and on time.

Computers and Law Enforcement

People working in the field of law enforcement use computers, too. In Lexington, Kentucky, for example, police officers use computers to respond to calls. When a call comes in to the dispatcher, a computer sends information to the police officer who will respond to the call. That information might include the name of the caller, an address, and other useful information.

Even a routine traffic stop can go more smoothly with the help of a computer. An officer can input a driver's license number to see if the person has any unpaid traffic tickets. The officer can also check the car's license plate to see if the vehicle is listed as stolen. If the person receives a ticket, the computer prints out the ticket. Because officers handle as many as twenty-five calls a shift, the time saved by computers allows the officers to take more calls.

Computers in a Police Cruiser

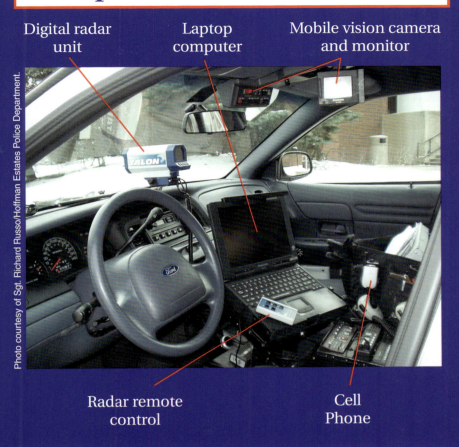

The FBI is another law enforcement agency that depends on computers to store and handle vast amounts of information. One system run by the FBI, the National Crime Information Center (NCIC), is a nationwide computerized information system available to police across the country. The system includes information about criminals and missing persons. Officers can compare information from crime scenes with information in the system to see if it matches crimes in other states. NCIC receives about 3.5 million police requests for information every day.

Computerized Medicine

The medical profession has also found many uses for computers. Doctors use computers to help diagnose illnesses. Medical workers in many fields rely on computers to store patient information.

Many tools for diagnosing illnesses rely on computers. One is the CAT scan. CAT stands for computerized axial tomography. The CAT scan uses computers to create three-dimensional images from two-dimensional X-ray pictures. A CAT scan can show an entire organ, such as the heart or brain, or it can show slices of the organ. This idea is similar to looking at a fruitcake from the outside. Someone looking at a fruitcake can see its overall shape, color, and texture. If that person slices the cake, the slice reveals many bits of nuts and fruits. Seeing inside an organ or a part of it helps doctors pinpoint problems and decide what must be done to fix them. All of this is done with the help of a computer.

When Christina Morgan was a high school senior, she felt a lump under her collarbone. Her doctor ordered several tests including a CAT scan. The CAT scan found a tumor around her windpipe. This tumor might not have been found without the combination of a computer and X-rays.

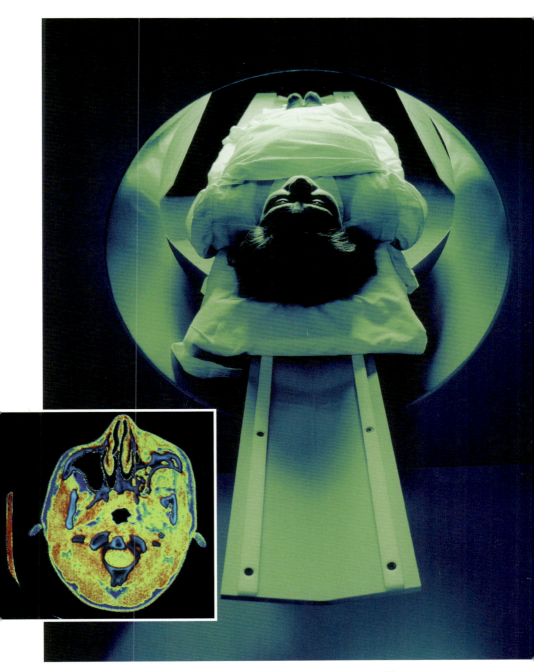

This woman is undergoing a CAT scan, which will create a computerized three-dimensional image of her brain.

Robots

Computers are found in many other work settings, too. Many of these computers operate other machines. Some combinations of computers and machines are called robots.

Robots do a lot of work in factories. Factory robots are built with metal "arms" and "hands" that turn and bend in different directions. Each robot is connected to a computer. The computer is programmed to make the robot do specific tasks. Usually these are repetitious tasks, or those that

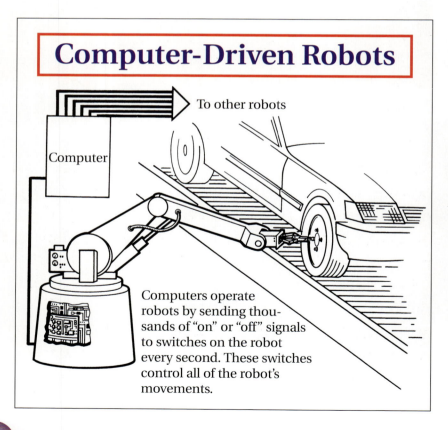

Computer-Driven Robots

To other robots

Computer

Computers operate robots by sending thousands of "on" or "off" signals to switches on the robot every second. These switches control all of the robot's movements.

Computerized robots at a Ford Motor plant in Canada weld pieces to a car with incredible speed and accuracy.

have to be done over and over again. Jobs such as bolting parts together are now often done by robots. Factory robots work more quickly than people can, and they cannot get hurt. They also do not get bored doing the same job over and over.

Human workers at the General Motors plant in Baltimore, Maryland, once did all the work of attaching fenders to car frames and installing windshields and other parts. Much of this work is now done by computerized robots. A computer tells a robot to pick up a bolt. Metal fingers on the

Computers at Work

On the far right of this picture, a Mars Rover can be seen studying a Martian rock (close-up, inset).

robot pick up the bolt, place it in the hole, and secure it. The robot arm has tiny motors that extend the arm and twist the joints. Sensors guide the arm to the hole in the car frame. The robot arm performs this job hundreds of times a day. The use of robots can free people to do more complicated and fulfilling tasks.

Robots also can do jobs that are dangerous for humans to do. Bomb disposal robots can detonate or turn off explosive devices. Some robots have been programmed to clean up toxic waste, so human workers will not be exposed to the hazardous materials. Robots also are used to repair oil pipelines under the ocean.

Space Explorers

One of the most exciting uses of robots as workers is in the field of space exploration. The Mars Rovers—

Spirit and Opportunity—arrived on Mars in January 2004. They spent about a year investigating the planet. These complicated robots were programmed to perform tasks such as drilling holes in rock, measuring the amount of chemicals in the dirt, and sending images back to Earth. Engineers on Earth were able to send commands to the rovers to change their direction or drill specific rocks.

People use computers in all types of work. Many jobs today could not be done without computers. Other jobs have been made easier, because computers do many repetitive or dangerous tasks so people do not have to.

Chapter 3

Computers for Fun

Many of the things people do for fun today involve a computer. Sometimes the role of the computer is easy to see, as when people play computer games or surf the Internet. In other cases, the computer is largely unseen. Special effects in movies and some animated films are made with the help of computers. However, audiences do not usually see these computers at work. Nor do people see the computer chips inside their television sets, DVD players, and CD players—but they are there. If they were not there, people would not be able to turn the channel, change song tracks, or record a television show.

Let's Play!

One of the most popular forms of entertainment today is the computer game. Many people play games on their desktop computers. Most computer games, however, are played on a video game console hooked up to a television or on a handheld device. Sony estimates that one out of four households in the United States owns a Sony Playstation game console. More than 172 million handheld Nintendo Game Boys have been sold since 1989.

Whatever the playing platform, computer games combine graphics and sound. High-speed processor chips power the games. Other computer hardware, such as video cards and graphic cards, provide the sights and sounds. Complicated software

A man plays a video game on a Playstation 2, a popular game console that operates using high-speed computer chips.

allows a player to play different versions of a game and save the results for another playing time.

Virtual Reality

As computers become faster and more powerful, the games become more realistic. Games that allow players to feel as if they are in the game are called **virtual reality**. Many of these games are found in arcades. In virtual reality programs, a player wears a headset or goggles and a glove to enter an artificial place. For example, one popular arcade game makes players feel as though they are in the driver's seat of a race car with a race track ahead of them. The headset allows players to experience the sounds and sights of the race as though they are part of real action. As players turn their heads, the images change to what they would see if the scene were real. The game shows other cars whizzing around the players' cars. The glove gives the players the sensation of grasping and moving objects such as a steering wheel. Sensors detect what the players' hands are doing and project that into the virtual world.

Very powerful computers and complicated software power virtual reality environments. Creating lifelike settings, sounds, and characters requires a lot of work with computers. Many of these same techniques are also used in movies.

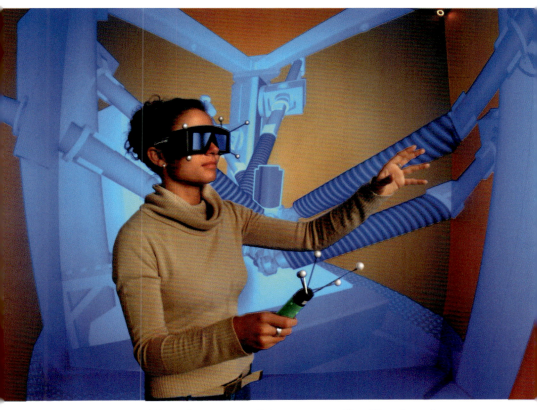

A computerized headset gives this woman the illusion that she is actually part of the action of a virtual reality game.

Animate This

Make-believe characters in movies seem real through the technology of computer animation. Computer artists produce the look and movement of characters, such as monsters and talking animals, to make them seem lifelike. One of the top computer-animation companies is Pixar Animation Studios. Pixar has produced movies such as *Toy Story, Finding Nemo,* and *A Bug's Life*.

Computer animation scenes begin as hand-drawn sketches that are then scanned into a computer.

A short computer-animated scene takes hours of work to make. First a hand-drawn storyboard maps out the events in the scene. Next, an animator sketches drawings of the main characters. Once the sketches are ready, they are scanned into the computer, and the computer creation begins.

Each character is plotted into the computer. Many points on the character's body are programmed into a grid so the computer can show how these points will move when the character moves. Woody from *Toy Story*, for example, has 100 sections just in his face so that it looks real when he talks or moves. If several characters are in a scene, each one must be sketched and plotted. Then software brings together the characters into one scene.

Once the movements of the characters are plotted and programmed, another programmer adds texture and light details to the scenes. Finally, sound is added to complete the movie. All this requires powerful computers and specialized animation software.

A programmer adds lifelike details to an animation scene in order to make it more believable.

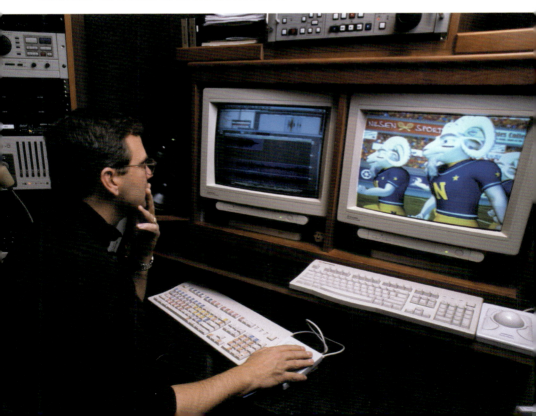

The same animation techniques can be used for special effects in movies. To show a tornado or tidal wave, a special effects expert studies movies of real tornadoes and tidal waves. Then he or she programs the movement and speed into a computer. The special effects can be blended into a scene with human actors or animated characters.

Travel Anywhere!

Another form of computer-generated fun is virtual travel. Although people may not have the time and money to travel to exotic places, they can visit them on their computers by way of the Internet.

Educational Web sites provide people a chance to see places they might not or cannot visit in person. The British Museum Web site shows displays of mummified animals from ancient Egypt and buried treasure from the oceans around Great Britain. Each month the museum features pictures of items from its collection of more than 5,000 objects. Pictures on France's Louvre Museum Web site allow people to enjoy the art of Leonardo da Vinci and many other artists. The Smithsonian National Air and Space Museum in Washington, D.C., puts a person in the pilot's seat for a 360-degree tour of more than 100 airplanes and spacecraft in its collection. More items are added to the tour each month.

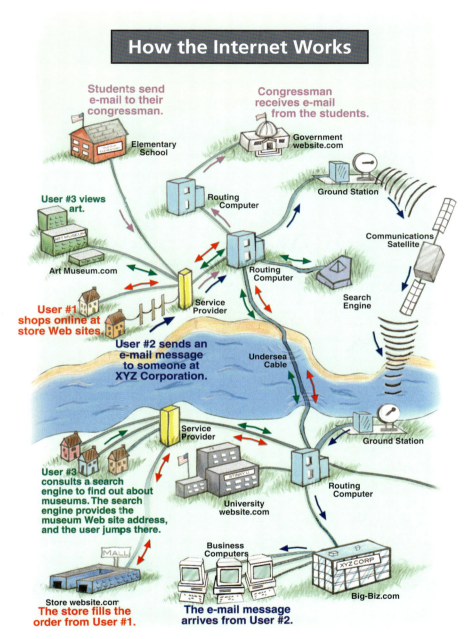

This chart shows how the Internet works. Follow the color-coded arrows and text to see how people communicate, shop, and view images from their computers through the Internet.

Computers for Fun 31

Cameras from around the world send images to the Web, allowing people to have many other travel experiences. The number of virtual travel sites increases daily. At the Panama Canal Web site, a person can watch the canal gates open and a ship move in as water fills the lock. NASA has several choices of space missions for people to observe on its official Web site. On other Web sites, people can tour the Taj Mahal in India and St. Paul's Cathedral in London.

As computer technology improves, people find more ways to use computers for entertainment. Playing games on a console or in virtual reality, going to movies, and taking a virtual trip on the Internet are all fun activities made possible with computers. New inventions will no doubt increase the use of computers for work and for fun.

Chapter 4

Super Fast, Super Powerful

Computers are a constant presence in our world. Their early development went very quickly. New ideas are still being tested, and some of these are rapidly advancing. More exciting inventions are ahead. In fact, some amazing ones are being developed now.

Even Faster and More Powerful

The most powerful computers today are called supercomputers. They can handle more than 1 trillion calculations a second. This is much faster than even the newest desktop computers. This speed is possible because several microprocessors are arranged so that data can be processed at the same time rather than in a specific order.

Supercomputers have many uses. Car makers use them to study car crashes. It would be very expensive to build a car with new safety features and then crash it to study what happens. By simulating, or imitating, the car and the crash on a supercomputer, designers can learn the same information. For example, if engineers want to design a safer air bag, they simulate the car crash with an air bag on a supercomputer and gather the information from the computer. Then they change the design of the air bag and simulate the crash again to see if the new design improves the air bag's safety.

Weather forecasters also rely on supercomputers. They can input many details about weather around

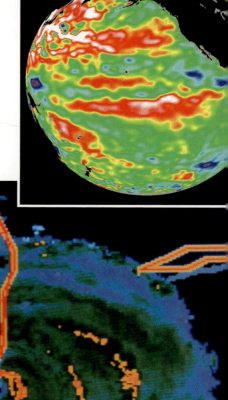

Weather forecasters use supercomputers to collect data from all over the world (right) to predict events like this hurricane in Florida (below).

the world. Then they use the computer's processing power to make predictions about the weather for days or even months ahead.

The Weather Service receives about 100 million weather observations a day. Everything from temperature, wind speed, and barometric pressure are input into supercomputers. Their super speed allows them to make about 450 billion calculations a second. It would take 123,000 people to do this same work. Out of this huge amount of information comes local and national forecasts. Supercomputers at the Climate Prediction Center in Camp Springs, Maryland, predicted a 45 percent chance of a very active Atlantic Ocean hurricane season for 2004. Four hurricanes hit Florida between August and September 2004, showing that computers can correctly predict weather.

More Uses for Supercomputers

Supercomputers are very expensive and have to be kept in a special cool environment so they can handle all those calculations. People could not afford to have a supercomputer at home, but more universities and companies are using them for projects that need super power. Projects such as researching genetics, predicting how national economies will grow, or managing information from space all may soon depend on supercomputers. Computers

NASA uses this supercomputer in a laboratory in California to help manage the data gathered by its space missions.

even faster than supercomputers may be developed soon.

Going with Light

The key to the advance of computers is light. Computers today run on electricity that passes through transistors and wiring built into the chips. Scientists are working on computers that would use light instead of electricity. Laser light can be beamed through tiny glass threads known as optical fibers. Most phone lines today are optical fibers that can carry thousands of phone conversations at one time. The next computers could use optical fibers to carry information.

Switches in optical computers would be 1,000 times faster than silicon transistors. Also, while silicon chips have to be flat, optical components can be made into any shape. One of the disadvantages of using electricity in computer chips is that signals sometimes get mixed up. Optical computers would not have this problem.

Really, Really Small

The field of study known as **nanotechnology** may bring about even smaller computers. Computers even smaller and faster than optical computers would have components the size of a few molecules. Molecules are groups of atoms, the smallest particles in any material. Scientists are working on switches and memory devices that would be made of only a few molecules. These switches would be about 60,000 times smaller than those in today's computers. Their tiny size would make them many times faster. These molecular switches could be combined to make nanocomputers.

Nanocomputers would be so small that hundreds of them could fit in the period at the end of this sentence. Even at such a small size, they could be programmed to do all sorts of amazing things. A patient could drink a mixture containing medical nanocomputers that would attack cancer cells or

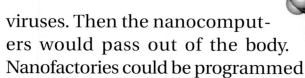

The field of nanotechnology is exploring the use of molecule-sized devices like these nanogears to create super-fast, tiny computers.

viruses. Then the nanocomputers would pass out of the body. Nanofactories could be programmed to manufacture products with no waste, because each item would be made exactly from atoms with nothing left over. Computers that small could be worn on the body, so a person would always have access to his or her medical files or information to keep from getting lost.

Nanocomputers would be several times more powerful than today's computers. More powerful computers would allow for more accurate weather forecasting and for any other use that requires a large amount of information. More uses for the nanocomputer would grow and change with the technology.

Artificial Intelligence

Computer scientists also are working on designing computers that operate in the same way as the human brain. This branch of computer science is called **artificial intelligence**. The brain does some tasks such as calculations at a slower pace than even a desktop computer does. However, the brain does two things better: It makes decisions and learns from its mistakes and successes.

Inside the human brain are tiny processors, similar to a computer. However, the organization of the brain allows it to work on several problems at once. A person may be walking to school, thinking about a test, and talking to a friend all at the same time.

A computer programmed with artificial intelligence identifies a customer of a Japanese bank by scanning his eyes.

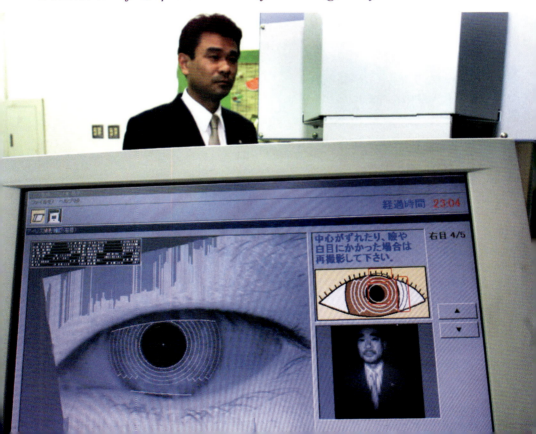

These humanoid robots represent the latest in artificial intelligence. They are programmed to play soccer with humanlike reflexes.

Scientists believe computers can be designed to accomplish tasks in more human ways. A brain-like computer could be trained to learn tasks. It might be taught to recognize faces or handwriting. Some of these computers are already being used by banks to approve loans and by chip designers to assist with the complicated layout of silicon chips. In the future, these computers might be used to identify criminals or allow access into high-security areas.

One problem that would have to be overcome is that the human brain is much more complex than any computer. The brain has 100 billion nerve cells, each connected to 10,000 other nerve cells. Today's computers are not able to copy these brain connections.

As computers become super fast and super powerful, people will find new uses for them. When computers were first being developed, people never imagined all the things they would be used for today. More than 50 years ago, Howard Aiken, an engineer and physicist, stated that six computers would satisfy the needs of the United States. In 1947, that seemed like a huge amount of computing power. In 2002, a research group estimated that 1 billion computers had been sold in the United States since 1975 and that another billion would be sold by 2007. These numbers include only desktop and laptop computers. They do not include all the computer chips in items such as cars, microwaves, and washing machines.

More uses for computers are developed every day, and faster and more powerful computers are coming soon.

Glossary

artificial intelligence: A branch of computer science that tries to make computers think and learn like humans.

hardware: The physical parts of a computer, such as the microprocessors, memory chips, printer, monitor, and keyboard.

icons: Pictures on a computer screen that activate a menu or application when clicked with the mouse.

integrated circuits: Combinations of transistors, connectors, and wires built from a single piece of silicon.

microprocessor: A single chip that contains memory and processing. It is called the computer on a chip.

nanotechnology: The study of changing molecules or atoms to make them into switches or machines.

software: The programs for a computer that are loaded into the computer and accessed when needed. Software tells the computer what to do.

transistor: A switch made of silicon that is used to perform the calculations needed by a computer.

vacuum tubes: Switches that controlled electrical current in early computers.

virtual reality: A combination of gear such as headsets and gloves run by a powerful computer that makes images seem real.

For Further Exploration

Books

Stephen Bennington, *All About Computers*. New York: Southwater, 2001. This book is filled with computer projects. Readers can make their own letterhead and newspaper, as well as design a computer game.

Preston Gralla, *Online Activities for Kids: Projects for School, Extra Credit or Just Plain Fun!* Hoboken, NJ: Wiley, 2001. This book is full of fun and educational online activities that kids can complete themselves.

Josepha Sherman, *The History of the Personal Computer*. Danbury, CT: Franklin Watts, 2003. Intriguing look into the lives of the inventors and developers of the personal computer.

Brian Williams, *Computers*. Chicago, IL: Heinemann Library, 2001. Interesting book that details how computers work and their history.

Web Sites

Apple Computer (http://ali.apple.com/ali_sites/ali/vft.php). This site has several interesting "field trips" and interactive programs about computers.

How Stuff Works (http://computer.howstuffworks.com). This site has articles about computer parts and how they work.

Intel (www.intel.com/intel/intelis/museum/index.htm). This site has interactive displays about microprocessors, transistors, and other computer parts.

Index

Aiken, Howard, 41
airline industry, 14–16
animation, 27–30
Apple Computers, 13
arcade games, 26
artificial intelligence, 38–41
automobile industry, 21–22, 33–34

Baltimore/ Washington International Airport, 15
Bell Labs, 6
bomb disposal, 22
British Museum, 30
Bug's Life, A (film), 27

cars, 33–34
CAT (computerized axial tomography) scans, 18
Climate Prediction Center, 35
computer chips, 4, 9

ENIAC, 4–6
e-tickets (electronic tickets), 14

factories, 20–22
FBI, 17–18
Finding Nemo (film), 27

games, 24–26

Gates, Bill, 13
General Motors, 21–22

hardware, 11, 25
Hopper, Grace Murray, 11
hurricanes, 35

integrated circuits, 4, 9

Jobs, Steve, 13

Kilby, Jack, 9

languages, 11, 12–13
lasers, 36–37
law enforcement, 16–18, 22
Lexington, Kentucky, 16
light, 36–37
Louvre Museum, 30

Macintosh computers, 13
Mars Rovers, 22–23
medical profession, 18
memory chips, 9
microprocessors, 9, 33
Microsoft, 13
Morgan, Christina, 18
mouse (computer), 13
movies, 27–30

nanoseconds, 9
nanotechnology, 37–38

NASA, 22–23, 32
National Crime
  Information Center
  (NCIC), 17–18
Nintendo Game Boys, 25
Noyce, Robert, 9

Opportunity (Mars Rover), 23
optical fibers, 36–37

Panama Canal, 32
pipeline repairs, 22
Pixar Animation Studios, 27
Playstation game consoles, 24–25
police, 16, 17–18, 22
processor chips, 9
programs, operation of, 11–13

robots, 20–23

sales, 41
silicon, 6, 9, 37
Smithsonian National Air and Space Museum, 30
software, 11, 25–26
space exploration, 22–23
speed, 9, 33
Spirit (Mars Rover), 23
supercomputers, 33–36
switches

molecular, 37
optical, 37
transistors, 6–7
vacuum tubes, 5

toxic-waste cleanups, 22
Toy Story (movie), 27, 29
transistors, 6–8, 36

uses
  airline industry, 14–16
  automobile testing, 33–34
  dangerous jobs, 22
  factories, 20–22
  games, 24–26
  law enforcement, 16–18, 22
  medical profession, 18
  movies, 27–30
  space exploration, 22–23
  virtual travel, 30, 32
  weather forecasting, 34–35

vacuum tubes, 5, 6, 7–8
virtual reality, 26
virtual travel, 30, 32

weather forecasting, 34–35
wiring
  transistors, 8, 36
  vacuum tubes, 5, 6
Wozniak, Stephen, 13

Picture Credits

Cover: © Ted Soqui/CORBIS
Stylianos Axiotis/EPA/Landov, 15 (below)
© Bettmann/CORBIS, 5 (both), 12
© CORBIS, 7
© CORBIS SYGMA, 8
© Mauro Fermariello/Photo Researchers, Inc., 40
© Henry Goskinsky/Time Life Pictures/Getty Images, 10
Lucent Books, 20
NASA, 22-23
NASA-HQ-GRIN, 36, 38
NASA-JPL, 34 (inset)
NOAA, 34 (below)
© Charles O'Rear/CORBIS, 19 (inset)
PhotoDisc, 10 (inset)
Photos.com, 15 (inset)
Fred Prouser/Landov, 25
© Reuters/CORBIS, 39
Photo courtesy of Sgt. Richard Russo/Hoffman Estates Police Dept., 17
Suzanne Santillan, 31
© Paul A. Souders/CORBIS, 21
Wolfgang Thieme/DPA/Landov, 27
© Bill Varie/CORBIS, 19
Gale Zucker/Blackbirch Press, 28 (both), 29

About the Author

Roberta Baxter wrote *Chemical Reaction,* also a KidHaven Science Library title. She has written articles about science and history for several magazines, as well as a teacher's guide on chemistry. She lives with her family in Colorado.